STANLEY SPENCER AT BURGHCLERE

The Oratory of All Souls
Sandham Memorial Chapel

Hampshire

National Trust

INTRODUCTION

BEFORE BURGHCLERE

Stanley Spencer was born in Cookham, Berkshire, on 30 June 1891. His upbringing as the eighth surviving child of William Spencer, a self-styled 'Professor of Music and Organist of St Nicholas, Hedsor,' was cheerfully unconventional by late Victorian standards. He and his younger brother Gilbert were taught by their older sisters in the 'school' which their father set up in a potting shed at the bottom of the garden. Isolated from all but their immediate surroundings, 'hidden bits of Cookham' were, according to Gilbert Spencer, 'as remote as the Milky Way'. Unlike their older siblings, Stanley and Gilbert Spencer turned not to music but to drawing and to painting. In 1908 Stanley Spencer led the way to the Slade School of Fine Art in London, where he became 'Cookham' to his fellow students, the incurable day student who travelled up to Waterloo on the 8.50 train each morning and returned again, with equal regularity, on the 5.08 pm.

At the Slade Spencer joined a remarkable class, one which included Paul Nash, David Bomberg, Mark Gertler, C.R.W. Nevinson and Edward Wadsworth. Among them, he shone, capturing the coveted Melville Nettleship Prize in 1912 with his painting of *The Nativity*. 'He has shown signs', Professor Henry Tonks wrote, 'of having the most original mind of anyone we have had at the Slade and he combines it with great powers of draughtsmanship.' It was generous praise indeed from someone who disapproved on principle of Post-Impressionism, neo-primitivism and, above all, of Gauguin, whose influence is clearly visible in the painting. By 1912, Spencer had also attracted approving attention from more advanced critics; Clive Bell included his small canvas of *John Donne Arriving in Heaven* (private collection) in the English section of Roger Fry's influential second Post-

The Nativity, 1912 (Slade School of Fine Art, University College London)

Travoys with Wounded Soldiers Arriving at a Dressing Station at Smol, Macedonia, 1919 (Imperial War Museum)

Impressionist exhibition, held at the Grafton Galleries in London. To the champions of modernism, its uncompromising simplicity pointed towards abstraction, although Spencer may well have also had early Italian painting in mind. The student group of artists known as 'the Primitives', of which Spencer was a member, admired Giotto, Masaccio and Fra Angelico. Ruskin wrote of the fourteenth-century Italian painter, 'Even in his smallest tempera pictures Giotto melted all these folds into broad masses of colour.' As for the setting, Heaven was, according to Gilbert Spencer, 'in this case a part of Widbrook Common'.

The triumphant graduate looked no further than Cookham for his first studio. He found it in Ovey's Barn, across the road from Fernlea, the family home in High Street. There, in a remarkable succession of paintings, he sought 'to bring the three experiences of my life together . . . the Slade with the life drawing . . ., the life at home, and the feeling the Bible gave me.' Like Samuel Palmer in Shoreham a century earlier, he felt 'fresh, awake and alive; this is the time for visitations . . . I leave off at dusk feeling delighted with the spiritual work I have done.'

That was written four years later, with understandable nostalgia, by Private Spencer on active service in the Royal Berkshire Regiment. Spencer spent the entire war in the ranks, first as a medical orderly at the Beaufort War Hospital near Bristol. Then, in August 1916, he volunteered for service overseas and was assigned to the 68th Field Ambulances in Macedonia. A year later he transferred to the 7th Battalion of the Berkshires, to spend several months in the front line before the fighting ended. Ironically, it was not the commission as an Official War Artist engineered for him in 1918 by his friends in England which rescued him, but a recurrence of the malaria he had contracted in Greece. By December 1918, Private Spencer was on leave in Cookham pending demobilisation, painting under orders *Travoys with Wounded Soldiers Arriving at a Dressing Station at Smol, Macedonia.* Privileged, as few of his fellow soldiers were, to return to the scenes of youth and early maturity, he attempted to recapture his pre-lapsarian vision by reviving the themes he had established before the war. He concentrated upon religious scenes, specifically upon a modern Passion cycle, with *Christ's Entry into Jerusalem* (1921; Leeds City Art Galleries), *The Last Supper* (1920; Stanley Spencer Gallery, Cookham), *The Betrayal* (1923; Ulster Museum, Belfast), and *Christ Carrying the Cross* (1920; Tate Gallery, London). For all of these, Cookham provided the setting, but when it came to the *Crucifixion* (1921; Aberdeen Art Gallery), Spencer chose a steep and barren mountainside. 'The memory I had of some mountain . . . dividing Macedonia from Bulgaria . . . as I walked towards the range . . . every sound was muffled . . . and only the faint jingle and squeaking of the mules' harnesses.'

Wartime memories continued to invade Spencer's artistic thoughts. In 1923, when he stayed in Dorset with the painter Henry Lamb, his host wrote that 'Stanley sits at a table all day evolving acres of Salonica and Bristol war compositions.' In his own words he had, by then, 'drawn a whole architectural scheme of the pictures', and with Lamb's encouragement he began to consider raising a subscription among his friends and patrons to enable him to realise the project. At that crucial moment, Mr and Mrs J.L. Behrend visited Lamb and Spencer. Mrs Behrend's brother, Lieutenant Henry Willoughby Sandham, had died in 1919 as a result of an illness he had contracted during the Macedonian campaign. Deeply impressed by Spencer's reminiscences of the same theatre of war, the Behrends decided, before the end of that summer, to commission Spencer's chapel as a private memorial. 'What ho, Giotto!' was his response.

In spite of Spencer's preference for a site in Cookham, the Behrends naturally chose to build their oratory near to their home in the Hampshire village of Burghclere. They appointed Lionel Pearson as their architect, with instructions to combine almshouses with Spencer's chapel, which was closely modelled by the painter upon Giotto's Arena Chapel in Padua. At first, Spencer thought of taking the analogy further, by painting in fresco, but after a series of experiments he wisely reverted to his familiar medium of oils on canvas.

While plans and building were under way, Spencer turned his attention to another major project. His painting of *The Resurrection, Cookham* measures 9 feet by 18 feet. In it, the painter paid tribute to his birthplace as the earthly paradise. It represents eternity in Cookham churchyard with Bond's steam launch full of day trippers happily careering past Redemption-on-Thames as Spencer welcomes his new circle of Hampstead friends, including Hilda Carline, whom he married in 1925, into the sacred groves of Cookham. The picture

The Resurrection, Cookham, 1924–5 (Tate Gallery)

Detail from *Ablutions* (3)

formed the centrepiece of the first one-man show Spencer held, at the Goupil Gallery in London, in February 1927. Fry hailed it as 'a very personal conception carried through with unfailing nerve and conviction' and it was bought for the Tate Gallery. A few weeks later, on 25 March, the Oratory of All Souls, Burghclere, was dedicated by the Bishop of Guildford. Coincidentally or not, the date of the Feast of the Annunciation was that on which Giotto's Arena Chapel had been consecrated some six centuries earlier.

BURGHCLERE

These paintings by Stanley Spencer and this oratory are the fulfilment of a design which he conceived whilst on active service 1914–18.

The inscription which Spencer had placed on the west wall of the Sandham Memorial Chapel identifies the scheme itself with wartime. When he learned, in May 1918, of his commission as an Official War Artist, he set to work not only on the design of *Travoys with Wounded Soldiers Arriving at a Dressing Station*, but also on a number of other compositions. Few of the drawings survive, but in his exhibition at the Goupil Gallery in 1927 he exhibited several oil sketches which he dated to 1919. At least two of them were to provide details for the scenes of encampment painted on the upper registers of the chapel. As such, they recur in the two studies which Spencer drew in 1923 to indicate the 'whole architectural scheme of the pictures'. These designs left little room for further architectural detailing, and Pearson incorporated into the building every one of Spencer's structural suggestions: for the sections of the mouldings, for the insertion of decorative corbels between the arches of the bay divisions, and for the curved dado beneath the 'predella panels' on the north and south walls.

Spencer did not wait for the building to be finished to begin painting. In 1927 he completed the first two small canvases destined for the chapel, *Scrubbing the Floor* (2) and *Sorting and Moving Kit-Bags* (4), in his studio in the Vale Hotel, Hampstead. In May, he and his wife moved with their baby

Study for the north wall, 1923 (Stanley Spencer Gallery, Cookham)

daughter Shirin to Burghclere where the Behrends arranged temporary accommodation for them at Palmer's Hill Farm. Meanwhile, his patrons were constructing not only the chapel but Chapel View, the house in which the Spencers lived with their servant Elsie until 1932. For the better part of four years, Spencer worked in the chapel itself. He painted as easel pictures the eight arch-topped canvases and the eight smaller 'predellas' which were installed into the bay divisions on the north and south walls. On the other hand, the uppermost sections of those walls, together with the entire east wall, had to be painted *in situ*. To minimise the number of seams, especially wide bolts of canvas were ordered from a Belgian manufacturer. The walls were first lined with asbestos cloth to which the lengths of canvas were then glued. During the summer of 1928 Mr Head, the builder, erected scaffolding in the chapel, from which Spencer could paint directly on to the canvas-covered walls.

In the course of working on the chapel, Spencer made a number of changes to the content and the order of the scenes proposed in his drawings of 1923. One of his earliest ideas for a painting based upon his service in the Royal Army Medical Corps was to represent an operating theatre. 'I should love to do a fresco of an operation,' he wrote to his friend Desmond Chute in 1916. 'And have the incision in the belly in the middle of the picture, and all the forceps radiating from it.' He illustrated the idea with a quick sketch which is repeated in the composition study for the north wall, as the third arched panel from the left. Ultimately, he rejected the subject altogether. In the chapel itself, he also re-ordered the scenes designed to occupy the main register of the south wall beginning with a new composition, *Reveille* (10), followed by *Filling Water-Bottles* (12; third in the drawing), *Map-Reading* (14; first in the drawing), and *Making a Fire-Belt* (16; greatly revised from the composition sketch for the second bay in the drawing).

Although each of the scenes on the north and south walls of the chapel illustrates some aspect of Spencer's own experience during the Great War, he avoided giving a straightforward, sequential account. His visual diary is arranged as a symbolic

Study for the south wall, 1923 (Stanley Spencer Gallery, Cookham)

narrative, as what he described as 'a mixture of real and spiritual fact'. In the lowest register, containing what Spencer referred to as 'predella scenes', seven of the eight canvases describe his duties as a medical orderly at the Beaufort War Hospital. Scrubbing floors, sorting laundry, and bedmaking provide the subjects for these modern equivalents to the 'labours of the months' in medieval art. To the students at the Ruskin School of Drawing in Oxford, Spencer explained in 1923 that 'ordinary experiences or happenings in life are continually developing and bringing to light all sorts of artistic discoveries . . . When I scrubbed floors, I would have all sorts of marvellous thoughts, so much that at last, when I was fully equipped for scrubbing – bucket, apron and "prayer mat" in hand – I used to feel much the same as if I was going to church.' His views derive from a long and respected tradition in Christian theology, from St Augustine's *Confessions*, 'ever busy, yet ever at rest . . .' to William Blake's discovery of 'eternity in a grain of sand'. Just one of the predella scenes, *Bedmaking* (15), treats Spencer not as an orderly but as a patient in the field hospital to which he was sent as a victim of malaria. Among the personal effects painted on to the wall behind one of the beds are photographs of Hilda Spencer, of their daughter Unity as a baby, of his father William Spencer standing in the porch of Hedsor Church, and other souvenirs of Spencer's own life.

As a counterpart to the hospital scenes below, Spencer described two unbroken panoramas above the bay divisions of the north and south walls – his life in the military encampments near the Macedonian front. *The Camp at Karasuli* (18) is depicted early in the morning; while some of the men cook breakfast over campfires, others have been detailed to carry stones for the construction of a road. Private Spencer appears in the foreground collecting litter with the point of a bayonet. On the opposite wall, in the *Riverbed at Todorovo* (19), duties are similarly divided between the group of soldiers on the riverbank, who make a red cross within a white circle out of carefully arranged stones, and those who do laundry at the water's edge. Perched on a rock in the foreground, in the spandrel between two of the arched bays, the muscular figure of a private scrubs away at a pair of undershorts. The analogy with the Sistine Ceiling is unavoidable as Spencer substitutes his own kind of hero, without the slightest hint of irony, for Michelangelo's Old Testament prophets. Rich in trivial incident and camp routine, the upper scenes provide vivid running commentaries upon life in the field as a backdrop for the eight carefully selected paintings 'of real and spiritual fact'.

In the first bay on the north wall, to the left of the chapel's entrance, Spencer painted a *Convoy Arriving with Wounded* (1). From his own first sight of Beaufort War Hospital, he recalled 'the gate was as massive and as high as the gate of hell. It was a vile cast-iron structure. Its keeper, though unlike that lean son of a hag who kept the gates of hell, being tall and thicker was nevertheless absolutely associated with that capricious . . . being who had charge of all the "deaduns" and did all the cutting up in all the post-mortem operations.' The implications are clear as the viewer enters the pictorial world of the chapel: it is an underworld, 'a dark and dreary Vale . . . and many a Region dolorous', through which the visual pilgrim must follow the painter's progress to find redemption. 'Before the Gates there sat/On either side a formidable shape'; the keeper and his assistant swing open the gates to raise the iron curtain upon the ensuing scenes. Like the soldiers aboard the bus, the visitor to the chapel is obliged to leave behind the sunshine and flowering rhododendron of the Berkshire countryside as Spencer observed and painted it during the summer of 1927. To underline the point, the corresponding predella (2), below the first scene, descends to the scarcely lit regions of the hospital's interminable corridors, in which figures of orderlies move in and out of the shadows with their trays of rations. To this dolorous scene, Spencer added from memory the figure of the shell-shocked soldier sprawled across the floor which he scrubs with obsessive concentration.

The progression is an obvious one, from the soap and water in the first bay to *Ablutions* (3) in the second. Here the orderlies assist their patients in the hospital washroom. Beneath, in the predella, their tasks continue as they act as porters to the patients. In *Sorting and Moving Kit-bags* (4) the emphasis is

John Louis Behrend; by Stanley Spencer, 1956 (Peter Nahum Ltd). Behrend and his wife commissioned Spencer to paint the Burghclere murals and owned the single largest collection of his works

upon service as well as routine. Spencer may well have recalled the words of the Psalmist: 'blessed be the man that provideth for the sick and needy: the Lord shall deliver him in the time of trouble.'

From Beaufort, the principal scene in the third bay moves to Tweseldown Camp, near Farnham, where Spencer was sent in 1915 for overseas training. *Kit Inspection* (5) depicts each of the men spreading out his groundsheet and laying out his kit according to army regulations. Each occupies his own small rectangular patch of earth, and if these figures are distantly reminiscent of the resurrected in Cookham churchyard, they anticipate far more clearly the contented beneficiaries of his Port Glasgow *Resurrections* (1945–50). In spite of Spencer's invariably cheerful interpretations of eternity, however, the analogy between a routine army inspection and the Day of Judgment remains uncomfortably plain, as each man prepares his account. In the corresponding predella (6), Spencer harks back to the Beaufort Hospital, and to another kind of assessment, as he and his fellow orderlies sort laundry into appropriate piles. From the rigours of field training, he may well have looked back with nostalgia to the relative domesticity of the hospital. As a juxtaposition in the chapel, *Sorting Laundry* (6) offers welcome relief from the painful symbolism of *Kit Inspection* (5).

The final scene on the north wall represents the front line. *Dug-out*, or *Stand-to* (7) is one of the most moving of the Burghclere paintings, in which the men who must fight the war emerge from their trenches into a landscape in which thickets of barbed wire replace the last vestiges of natural vegetation. No other war artist painted a scene of greater desolation, which Spencer rendered all the more poignant by treating it as the barren setting for his hapless comrades. The figure of the sergeant, in the left foreground, is based upon a drawing of a *Camouflaged Grenadier* (Tate Gallery), a recollection by Spencer of a particularly daring soldier who was killed in action. Once again, the trenches cut into the crust of the earth are like graves; the entire scene operates at that ambiguous level of the real and the spiritual in which the artist operated. 'The idea', he wrote, 'occurred to me in thinking how marvellous it would be if one morning, when we came out of our dug-outs, we found that somehow everything was peace and that war was no more . . . It is a sort of cross between an "Armistice" picture and a "*Resurrection*".' Beneath, in the subterranean vaults of the hospital, the orderlies continue their drudgery, *Filling Tea Urns* (8), as yet unredeemed, but by their very actions, 'bearing, filling, guarding', redeemable.

Dug-out provides the necessary transition to the focal point of the entire chapel, its east wall, covered by a vast battle-scarred landscape for *The Resurrec-*

tion of the Soldiers (9). As early as 1923, Spencer had determined to devote 'the end wall . . . to . . . a tall circular topped picture of . . . the resurrection of the soldiers in Salonica.' In 1927, he wrote to Richard Carline that he was thinking of 'filling the whole end wall with barbed wire', but shortly afterwards he made the study in which he gave prominence to the figure of Christ seated impassively in front of the risen soldiers who stack their crosses around him. The foreground remained a problem; yet another study (now lost) proposed fallen soldiers at eye level, sprawling in ungainly confusion towards the spectator. Happily that was abandoned in favour of the brilliant solution which Spencer began to paint *in situ* in the autumn of 1928. The figures behind the altar are almost life-size. The pictorial space they occupy is a continuation of that of the chapel itself, so that they confront the viewer as undeniable presences, recalled to life and redeemed amidst the symbols of their sacrifice. On his journey across Europe in 1922, when he travelled back to the scenes of his wartime experiences, Spencer must have seen those vast military cemeteries planted with forests of simple, white-painted wooden crosses, each one marking the mortal remains of a fallen soldier. He chose to paint them not in neat, graveyard rows but on the Day of Judgment, uprooted by their owners and piled as tokens of their sacrifice throughout the landscape and down, so that they appear to rest upon the actual altar of All Souls. The east wall fulfils the promise of a new dawn: reincarnation replaces the fury of war, the frustrations of life in the ranks, and human suffering, even unto death. 'The Burghclere memorial', Spencer wrote, 'redeemed my experience from what it was; namely something alien to me. By this means I recover my lost self.'

Turning to the south wall, *Reveille* (10) corresponds to *Dug-out* (7). 'I shall try', Spencer wrote to Richard Carline, 'to express the fact that . . . the idea is, again, the Resurrection. The men looking in the door of the tent are clearly doing nothing and are free from any hurry . . . the underlying intention is a great feeling of peace and happiness.' Like any good composer, Spencer recognised the value of a change in tempo. After building to the climax of the Resurrection, he must have felt the need for a slow movement, with softer tones and more lyrical passages. The comfortably enveloping folds of the mosquito nets in *Reveille* find a counterpart in the billowing bedclothes of the hospital scene below, in which Spencer recalled treating patients with frostbite. Next comes *Filling Water-Bottles* (12). In this, the figures of the soldiers almost appear to float, their capes billowing like vestments as they reach out for the water which sustains them. It is hard to resist a liturgical interpretation of this scene of relief and refreshment, especially when it is accompanied, in the predella below, by the domestic equivalent of the feeding of the five thousand, *Tea in the Hospital Ward* (13). In the third bay *Map-Reading* (14) continues the theme: 'He shall feed me in a green pasture: and lead me forth beside the waters of comfort.' The landscape in which the soldiers rest as their commanding officer pores over his map of the region is lush and welcoming. 'Resting and contemplating' were the activities Spencer intended to convey in a scene which reinstates the natural world as a source of human comfort. Thc idea of recuperation is continued below, in the hospital scene which refers to Spencer's own convalescence.

Finally, in 1932, Spencer painted *Making a Fire Belt* (16) as the last of the main scenes to occupy the south wall. The resemblance to the artist of the figure crouching in the foreground is unmistakable and confirms his statement that 'all my figures are simply "me", putting myself in places and circumstances in which I want to be'. At the centre of the composition, five Spencer-like figures are arranged as though they were pivoted from a central axis to form an emblematic representation of physical effort. Beneath in the predella, Spencer reinforced the point with *Washing Lockers* (17), a reminiscence of the bathtubs at the Beaufort Hospital which was especially important to him. 'I have only to mentally place myself between the baths to feel at once inspired,' he explained. In the final bay he comes full circle, returning to his original premise; 'and so it came about, at last, that tea-rooms, bathrooms, beds, etc. all became sort of symbols of my spiritual thoughts until at last I felt I could reveal the whole progress of my soul by stating clearly these impressions of my surroundings.'

AFTER BURGHCLERE

Spencer completed the chapel decorations in 1932. By then he and his family had moved back to Cookham, where he painted the last of the canvases in his new studio there. Meanwhile, his reputation as a painter continued to grow. In the same year he was elected an Associate of the Royal Academy, and he was invited to show ten works in the British Pavilion at the Venice Biennale. In 1933, his painting of *Sarah Tubb and the Heavenly Visitors* received honourable mention in the Carnegie Institute's International Exhibition in Pittsburgh, USA. To the book on *English Painting* he published in 1933, R.H. Wilenski added an appendix on 'The Burghclere Memorial Chapel', claiming Spencer as the true successor to the Pre-Raphaelites. In his admiration Wilenski sought to identify Spencer with a specifically native tradition, going back to Hogarth as the great narrative painter and Blake as its visionary. The comparisons are both flattering and telling, yet they have until recently encouraged critics to see Spencer as isolated from the mainstream of twentieth-century European art. However, in 1933 he evidenced in his figure style that tendency towards simplified volume which is common to the work of the same date by Henry Moore and William Roberts. His portraits, with their sharp focus and unflinching intimacy, recall the work of Christian Schad and other artists of the Neue Sachlichkeit, while his *Beatitudes of Love* (1937–8), for long regarded as indecent eccentricities, are closer to the work of German Expressionism in general and Max Beckmann in particular, than any other English painting of the same period.

The Sandham Memorial Chapel has no immediate heirs in the history of English mural painting. Painters such as Duncan Grant knew and admired it, but in their own decorative schemes they were more inclined towards Matisse. And Spencer's own plans for a sequel never materialised. From 1932 onwards, in his own words, 'all the figure pictures . . . were part of some scheme, the whole of which scheme when completed would have given the part the meaning I know it had.' His ambition was to build in Cookham a temple to his faith in universal love. 'During the war,' he wrote, 'when I contemplated the horror of my life and the lives of those with me, I felt the only way to end the ghastly experience would be if everyone suddenly decided to indulge in every degree and form of sexual love.' To what he readily admitted was 'a chapel in the air', he assigned mentally all of his subject pictures. In doing so, he created a kind of gallery of the mind; it is important to remember that even the largest of his later canvases remained easel paintings as distinct from murals. For that reason alone, within Spencer's own work, the Sandham Memorial stands in isolation.

Perhaps if Spencer had attracted industrial patronage, as the Mexican Diego Rivera succeeded in doing during the 1930s, his influence might have spread. In 1929 he did receive one, initially promising commission from the Empire Marketing Board to produce a series of designs for posters to promote the value of *Industry and Peace*. Spencer responded immediately. His first proposal, for two large works, was rejected in favour of five easel paintings which he duly completed and the Board just as promptly consigned to storage. In the face of that kind of reception, it is hardly surprising that he preferred to pursue his own, more private vision of a better world. Ironically, it took another war to rescue Spencer from a decade of introspection. During the Second World War he was again appointed an Official War Artist, and in may 1940 he made his first expedition to Lithgow's Shipyards in Port Glasgow. There, once again surrounded by teeming, toiling humanity, he rediscovered his affection for his fellows as individual men and women, bound together by their common tasks. 'I felt as disinclined to disturb them', he wrote, 'as I would be to disturb a service in a church.' In many ways Port Glasgow was Spencer's sequel to Burghclere.

DUNCAN ROBINSON

THE CHAPEL PAINTINGS

1 *Convoy Arriving with Wounded*

This was the first picture to be painted in the chapel itself. It shows a convoy of wounded soldiers arriving at the Beaufort War Hospital, Bristol. The ugly, thick-set warder in the right foreground was an unpleasant character who frightened Spencer. His keys are the same as those used for the chapel doors at Burghclere. The rhododendrons crowding in on the scene are a local introduction inspired by the lanes round Burghclere, and Spencer used them to disguise the details of the hospital drive which he could not clearly recall. This painting immediately sets the tone of the whole Burghclere cycle – that of the human companionship of war, not the horror of the front-line action.

2 *Scrubbing the Floor*

One of the first pictures, painted in Hampstead in 1927. A shell-shocked man in a corridor of the Beaufort Hospital is scrubbing the floor and has an obsessive way of throwing himself down to do the work. The drab, featureless walls are deeply evocative of this depressing institution where Spencer began his wartime service.

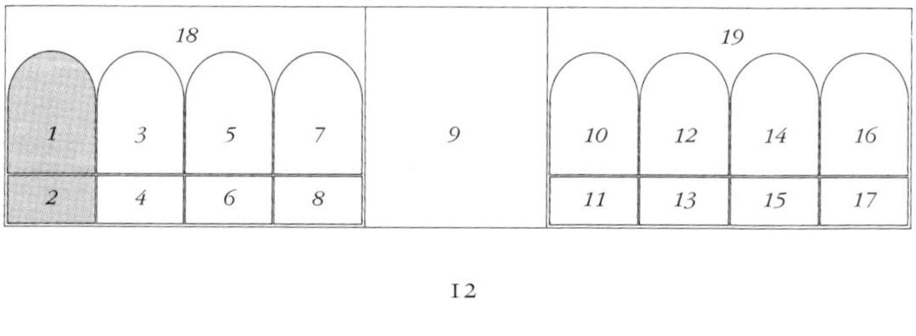

18					19			
1	3	5	7	9	10	12	14	16
2	4	6	8		11	13	15	17

3 *Ablutions*

In the centre an orderly is painting a soldier with iodine; behind him another soldier pulls on his braces, while others wash, dry and dress. All the pathos of military hospital life is summed up in the dedicated manner in which a second orderly is polishing the basin taps. Spencer regarded the mundane activities of the hospital with a sense of religious ritual, and the hospital pictures symbolise a quotation from St Augustine's *Confessions*: '. . . ever busy yet ever at rest, gathering yet never needing; bearing; filling; guarding; creating; nourishing; perfecting.'

4 *Sorting and Moving Kit-Bags*

This picture was also painted in Hampstead in 1927, before the artist moved to Burghclere to work in the chapel itself. The scene depicts a newly arrived convoy in the background pointing out their padlocked kitbags to the hospital orderlies. The drab colours and stark architecture again help to evoke a cold, cheerless institutional scene.

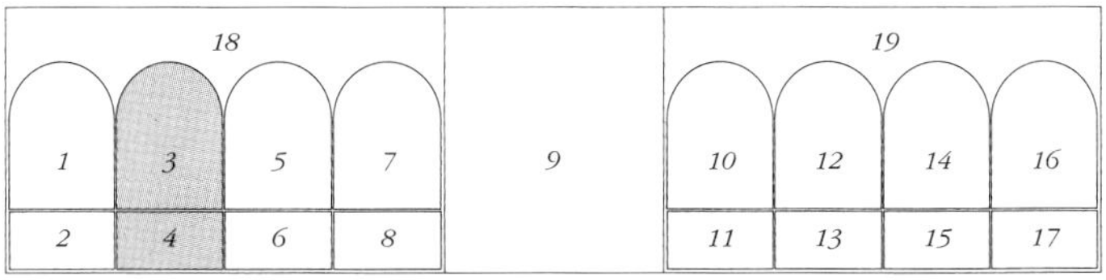

5 *Kit Inspection*

To an untidy, unmaterialistic man like Spencer, a kit inspection must have been an irksome business, but on a different plane he was undoubtedly fascinated by the idea of soldiers surrounded by their own little world of trite everyday objects. The scene is set at Tweseldown Camp, near Farnham in Surrey, where Spencer was transferred from Beaufort Hospital for basic training before leaving for Macedonia.

6 *Sorting the Laundry*

This is another domestic scene, much more cheerful than some of the preceding ones. The supervisor this time is a nurse in a clean, crisp uniform rather than a bullying NCO, and the happier spirit is reflected in the bustle of activity. The spotted handkerchiefs belonged to the permanent inmates of Beaufort, which was a mental hospital temporarily taken over by the military.

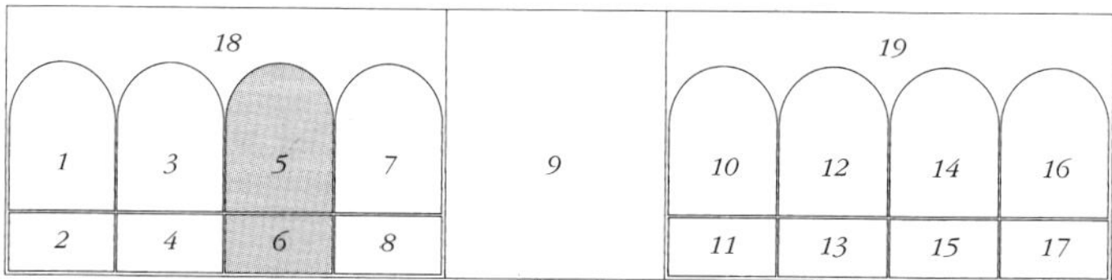

7 *Dug-out (or Stand-to)*

Spencer now transports us for the first time to the Salonika front, in Macedonia. He intended the thunder-cloud pattern of barbed wire to indicate a contrast between the threatening atmosphere of this scene and the relative domesticity of the preceding scenes. As they emerge from the trenches, the expressions of weariness and fear in the soldiers' faces, except that of the sergeant in the foreground, make this the most intense scene in the series. But the tension is relieved as some of the men realise what is happening behind them: they are looking beyond death towards the Resurrection on the east wall.

8 *Filling Tea Urns*

The final predella scene on the north wall continues the hospital theme of the previous three. Here the dark life of the mental patients, which fascinated Spencer, is hinted at by the solitary figure on the far side of the counter filling an urn for one of the hospital wards, while the orderlies collect their tea for the military wards.

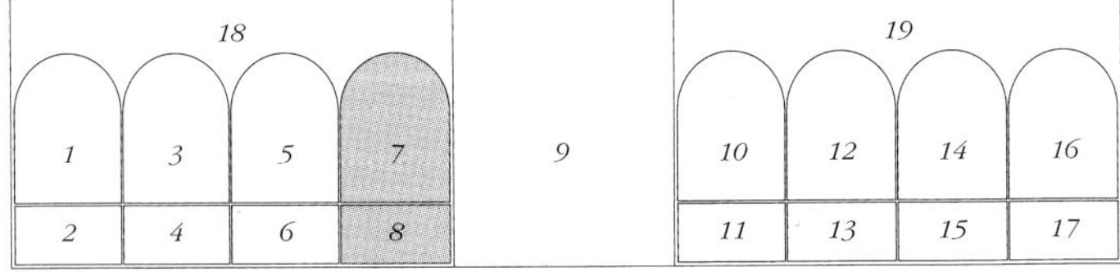

9 *The Resurrection of the Soldiers*

The *Resurrection* took Spencer nearly a year to complete. It dominates the chapel and all the other scenes are subordinate to it. The picture is a reminder of the relationship between war, death and Christianity, not merely a convenient and familiar religious image behind the altar. The composition is based on a complex pattern of wooden crosses which was suggested to Spencer by his habit of squaring up the canvas in order to work out the design. As a living soldier hands in his rifle at the end of service, so a dead soldier carries his cross to Christ, who is seen in the middle distance receiving these crosses. Spencer's idea was that the cross produces a different reaction in everybody.

The centre of the picture is dominated by a collapsed waggon, which was based on Spencer's recollection of a dead Bulgarian mule team and ammunition limber. Mules left a deep impression on the artist and are a constant theme in the Macedonian pictures. Here the dead mules and their handler come back to life and turn towards the figure of Christ. On the waggon boards lies a young soldier intently studying his cross and the figure of Christ represented on it.

The foreground is related to the position of the altar and intended to form a subject in itself – 'a sort of portrait gallery formed by soldiers coming out of the ground and the crosses arranged so as to look like frames'. The soldiers are emerging from their graves behind the altar, shaking hands with their resurrected comrades, cleaning buttons and winding puttees.

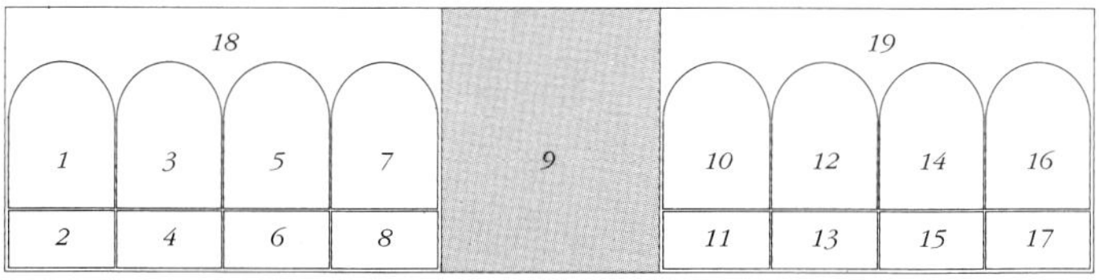

10 *Reveille*

Soldiers are dressing and shaving under mosquito nets, when their companions look in to tell them that the war is over. The idea of Reveille is the physical equivalent to Resurrection, and the picture connects with *Dug-Out* (7), occupying the same position in relation to the east wall; both scenes were originally thought of as part of the *Resurrection* picture. On a spiritual plane the soldiers on the right have perhaps seen the truth of the Resurrection and are eager to inform their colleagues.

11 *Frostbite*

Another of the ward scenes set in Beaufort War Hospital. Scraping the patients' feet was one of Spencer's tasks. In the background beds are being made and mattresses turned.

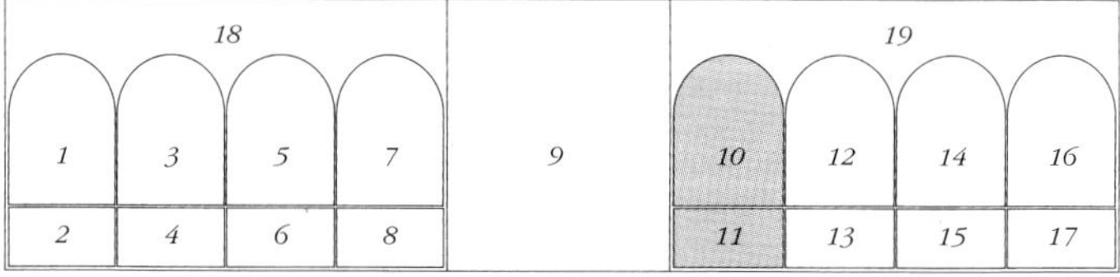

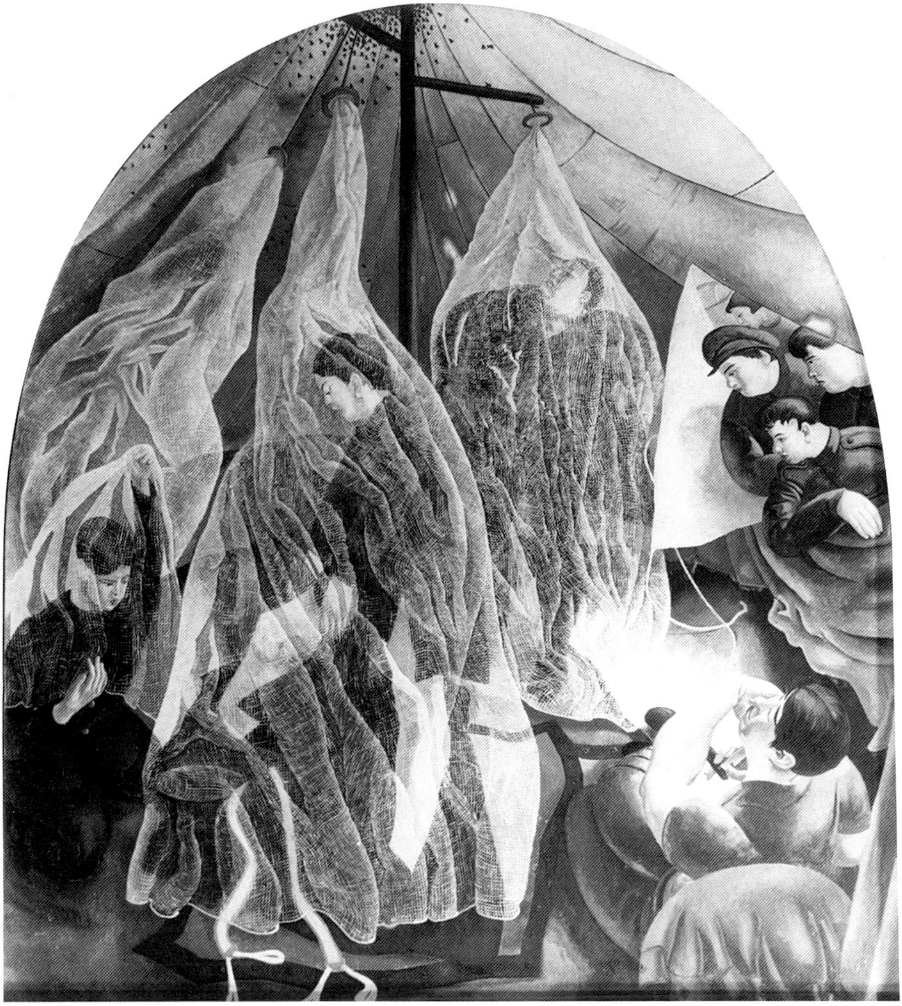

12 *Filling Water-Bottles*

The soldiers are wearing topis and army mackintoshes. Once again two mules dominate the foreground, balancing the soldiers high up on the rocks who are gathering water from the stream-fed fountain.

13 *Tea in the Hospital Ward*

This scene did not figure in the original cartoon for the series and was the last of the predella canvases to be painted, in 1932. There is a story that, after his identity became known to the Matron at Beaufort, there was always more bread and jam on Spencer's ward, as this was the artist's own favourite diet.

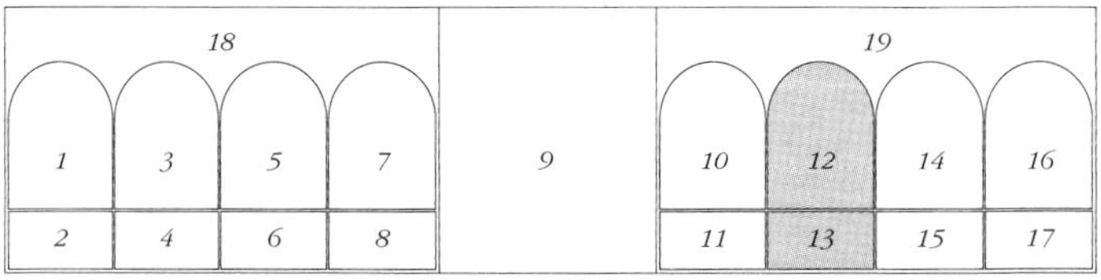

18

1 3 5 7

2 4 6 8

9

19

10 12 14 16

11 13 15 17

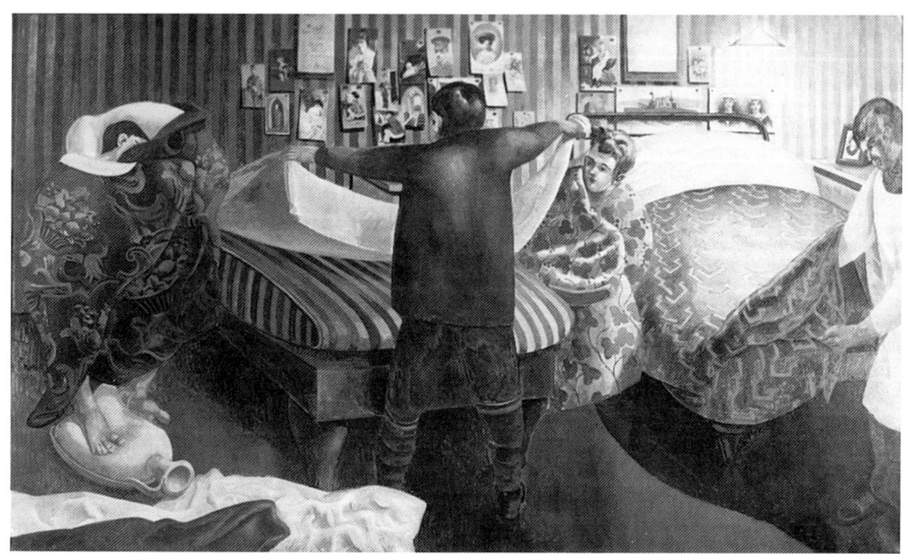

14 *Map-Reading*

The men are resting or picking bilberries during a pause in a route march. The officer, the only one to appear in the chapel cycle, consults his orders and map, while his horse is fed from a nose-bag. On the map Spencer included all the places he could remember visiting in Macedonia.

15 *Bedmaking*

This shows a hospital ward in a requisitioned house in Salonika, to which Spencer was sent as a patient when taken ill with malaria. His wife Hilda is one of the pin-ups above the beds, and another is of Spencer's father at the door of Hedsor Church, where he was organist.

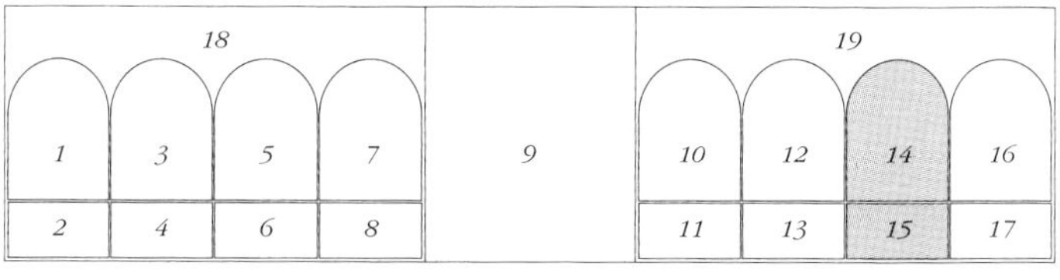

18 19
1 3 5 7 9 10 12 14 16
2 4 6 8 11 13 15 17

16 *Firebelt*

The grass is being burnt off round the evening camp to create a protective fire barrier. The soldiers are using spills, made from pages of the *Balkan News*. The figure crouching in the foreground is a portrait of the artist.

17 *Washing Lockers*

A bathroom at Beaufort Hospital. Spencer used to hide himself between the baths in order to escape tiresome duties or simply to work alone and undisturbed.

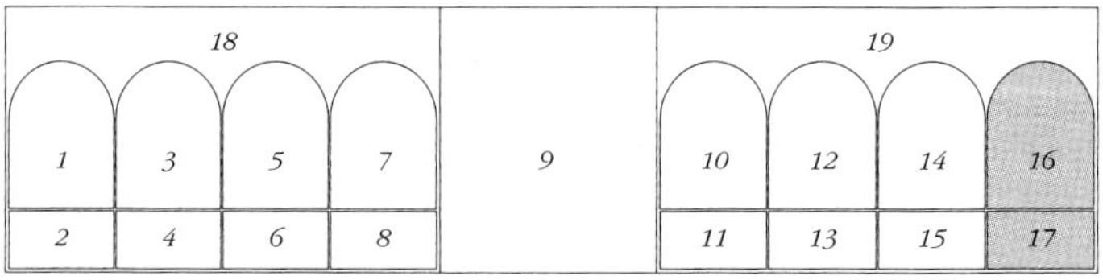

ABOVE LEFT AND RIGHT:

18			
1	3	5	7
2	4	6	8

18 *Camp at Karasuli (North Wall)*

The camp is shown in early morning. Men are cooking breakfast or carrying stones for the Serres military road, which is winding through the background of the picture. Another man – Spencer himself – is collecting discarded newspaper (*The Balkan News*).

BELOW LEFT AND RIGHT:

19 *Riverbed at Todorovo (South Wall)*

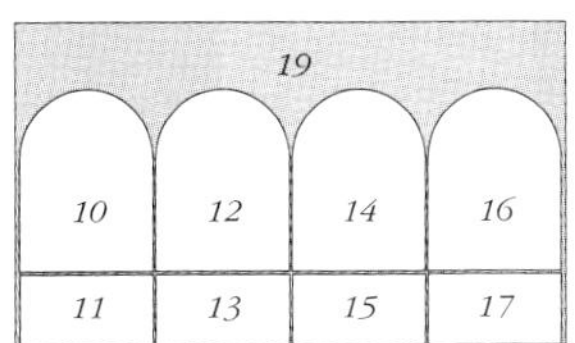

Some of the soldiers are playing housey-housey, while others are making patterns out of pebbles, including, on the left, the badges of the Royal Army Medical Corps and the Royal Berkshires, the regiments in which Spencer served.

BIBLIOGRAPHY

BEHREND, George, *Stanley Spencer at Burghclere*, London, 1965

BELL, Keith, *Stanley Spencer*, Royal Academy, 1980

CARLINE, Richard, 'New Mural Paintings by Stanley Spencer', *Studio*, lxlvi, Nov 1928, pp. 316–23

CARLINE, Richard, *Stanley Spencer at War*, London, 1978

COLLIS, Maurice, *Stanley Spencer*, London, 1962

POPLE, Kenneth, *Stanley Spencer*, London 1991

ROBINSON, Duncan, 'The Oratory of All Souls, Burghclere', *Stanley Spencer*, Arts Council, 1976

ROBINSON, Duncan, *Stanley Spencer*, Oxford, 1979 [revised edition, 1990]

ROTHENSTEIN, John, *Modern English Painters II, Lewis to Moore*, London, 1956, pp.180–4

WILENSKI, R.H., *English Painting*, London, 1933, pp. 280–5

THE CHAPEL FURNISHINGS

Many admirers of Spencer have contributed to the furnishings of the chapel. The former Rector of Burghclere, the late Rev. Canon R.S. Medlicott, gave a set of vestments and handsomely bound attendance book. R.E. Enthoven, FRIBA, designed the corbels for the arches. Lord Justice Slesser gave the altar cross.

THE STANLEY SPENCER GALLERY, COOKHAM

Kings Hall, Cookham on Thames, near Maidenhead and the M4

The only memorial gallery in Britain devoted to an artist in the village of his birth. This unique gallery is housed in a chapel to which Spencer's mother took him to Sunday School. It was renovated, furnished and is maintained entirely by voluntary contributions. In addition to its own acquisitions the gallery includes from time to time paintings on loan from public and private collections. As well as the paintings and drawings there are letters, photographs and objects intimately associated with the artist's working life. Close to the gallery, situated in the picturesque village which Spencer immortalised, are Fernley, where the artist was born, and the ancient church of Holy Trinity, Cookham, where a copy of Spencer's *The Last Supper* hangs; the original is in the gallery.

'The Friends of the Stanley Spencer Gallery' assist in the running of the gallery. Membership is open to everyone. Members receive a season ticket for the gallery valid for one year and participate in outings and other events to promote a wider and more informed interest in Spencer's works. From time to time they assist in the acquisition of additions to the permanent collection, and are archivists to the gallery. They contribute to funds for improvements and maintenance of the gallery. There are reduced rates for students and groups. Applications for membership and donations to funds should be sent to the Hon. Treasurer: G.R. Brown, Linnets, Terry's Lane, Cookham, Berkshire SL6 9RT.